Ace the Executive IT Interview

Real Executive IT Interview Questions with the Best Example Answers

MATT OLIVIER

Matt Olivier

Ace the Executive IT Interview

Table of Contents

Ace the Executive IT Interview

Ch. 1 Introduction

An executive IT interview is a crucial step in the process of securing a leadership position in the technology field. It is an opportunity for the interviewer to gain a better understanding of your qualifications and experience, as well as your ability to lead and manage teams and projects.

Preparing for an executive IT interview is essential for making a good first impression and demonstrating your knowledge, skills, and abilities. It allows you to highlight your relevant experience, communicate your vision and strategy, and show that you are a strong leader and problem solver.

During the interview, the interviewer will also be evaluating your communication skills, ability to work under pressure and your ability to think strategically. By preparing beforehand, you can anticipate and address any concerns the interviewer may have and demonstrate your readiness for the role.

Overall, preparing for an executive IT interview is crucial for effectively communicating your qualifications and demonstrating your ability to lead and manage technology projects and teams. It will give you the edge to stand out among the other candidates and increase your chances of landing the job.

Ch. 2 Understanding the Company and its Strategy

Understanding the company and its strategy is crucial for aligning technology projects with the overall business goals. It's important to research the company and its history, its products and services, its target market and customers, its competition, and its overall business strategy. This information can be gathered from the company's website, annual reports, industry publications, and other publicly available resources.

During the interview process, it's important to demonstrate that you have taken the time to research the company and understand its strategy. This can be done by asking informed questions about the company and its strategy during the interview, and by relating your own experience and skills to the company's specific needs and goals.

It's also important to understand the company's internal culture, its decision-making process, and the key stakeholders involved in technology projects. Understanding these factors will help you to navigate the company's internal politics and effectively communicate and align the technology project with the overall business strategy.

In summary, understanding the company and its strategy is crucial for aligning technology projects with the overall business goals. It's important to research the company and its history, its products and services, its target market and customers, its competition, and its overall business strategy. By understanding the company's culture, decision-making process, and key stakeholders, you can align your technology projects with the company's overall business strategy and achieve success.

2a. How to research a company and its technology strategy.

To research a company and its technology strategy, you can start by visiting the company's website and reviewing their mission statement, values, and overall business strategy. You can also review their annual reports, which will provide information about their financial performance and technology investments.

You can also research the company's technology strategy by reading industry publications and articles, such as trade journals and technology blogs. This will give you a sense of the company's position in the industry and the technology trends they are following.

Another way to research a company's technology strategy is to look at their patents and research publications. This will give you an idea of the technology they are developing and the areas they are investing in.

You can also look at the company's competitors, and see how they are positioning themselves in the industry and what technology they are investing in. This will give you an idea of how the company's technology strategy compares to others in the industry.

It's also a good idea to speak with industry experts and professionals who are familiar with the company and its technology strategy. They can provide valuable insights and perspective on the company's technology strategy and the industry as a whole.

Finally, you can also attend industry conferences and events where the company is presenting or exhibiting. This will give you the opportunity to learn more about the company's technology strategy and speak with their representatives.

Overall, researching a company and its technology strategy requires a combination of different methods, such as visiting their website, reading industry publications, and speaking with experts, and attending events. By gathering information from various sources, you can gain a comprehensive understanding of the company's technology strategy and align your own skills and experience with their goals.

2b. Understanding the company's culture and mission.

Understanding a company's culture and mission is important for aligning technology projects with the overall business strategy. The company's culture and mission will provide insight into the company's values, goals, and priorities, which will inform the approach and direction of the technology project.

To understand a company's culture and mission, you can start by reviewing the company's website, mission statement, and values. You can also read about the company's history, and the people and leaders behind the company. This will give you an understanding of the company's origins, philosophy, and what is important to the company.

You can also speak with current or former employees, or people who have worked with the company, to gain insight into the company's culture and mission. They can provide valuable information about the company's values, goals, and priorities, as well as the internal politics and decision-making process.

Another way to understand a company's culture and mission is to attend company events such as open houses, networking events, and employee engagement activities. This will provide an opportunity to observe the company's culture, meet employees, and learn more about the company's values, goals, and priorities.

It's also important to understand how the company's culture and mission align with the overall technology strategy. For example, if the company values innovation and agility, the technology strategy should reflect those values by investing in new technologies and agile methodologies.

Overall, understanding a company's culture and mission is important for aligning technology projects with the overall business strategy. By researching the company's history, values, and goals, and speaking with current and former employees, you can gain a comprehensive understanding of the company's culture and mission and align your technology project with the company's overall strategy.

2c. Identifying key technologies used by the company.

Key technologies used by a company can vary depending on the industry and specific products or services offered by the company. Some common technologies used by many companies include:

- Cloud computing platforms, such as Amazon Web Services (AWS), Microsoft Azure, or Google Cloud Platform (GCP)

- Programming languages and frameworks, such as Java, Python, JavaScript, and .NET

- Database management systems, such as MySQL, MongoDB, and PostgreSQL

- Machine learning and artificial intelligence technologies

- Cybersecurity technologies, such as firewalls, intrusion detection and prevention systems, and encryption

It's important to note that the specific technologies used by a company will depend on their specific needs and the industry they operate in.

Ch. 3 What Types of Answers Executive Employers are looking for

When asking you executive IT interview questions, the employer is looking for your ability to demonstrate your technical and leadership skills, as well as your ability to navigate and solve complex problems. They want to see that you have the experience and knowledge to approach and manage risks, handle resistance to change, balance conflicting priorities, align technology projects with the overall business strategy, build and maintain relationships with key stakeholders, evaluate and improve team performance, navigate a complex regulatory environment, and manage vendor and third-party risks.

When answering these questions, it's important to provide specific examples from your experience to demonstrate your abilities. Emphasize your achievements and results, and how you used critical thinking and problem-solving skills to overcome challenges. Be sure to communicate your understanding of the industry regulations and standards, and how you've applied them in your previous roles.

It's also important to show that you have the ability to lead, communicate and manage effectively, and that you can motivate and lead teams to achieve results. Show your ability to think strategically and how you've made decisions that are aligned with the overall business strategy, and how you've handled personnel issues in a professional and constructive way.

Overall, the employer wants to see that you have the qualifications, experience, and skills necessary to be successful in an executive IT role, and that you can lead, manage, and deliver results for the company.

3a. Use the STAR method.

The STAR method stands for (Situation, Task, Action, Result) and is a structured approach to answering behavioural and situational interview questions. It helps you to provide specific examples of your past experiences and how they align with the position and company. The STAR method is an acronym that stands for:

- Situation: Describe the background or context of the situation you were in. This could be a specific project you worked on, a problem you were trying to solve, or a challenge you faced.

- Task: Explain the task or goal you were trying to accomplish. This could be a specific deliverable you were responsible for or a problem you were trying to solve.

- Action: Describe the actions you took to accomplish the task or goal. Be specific about your role and responsibilities and what you did to achieve the desired outcome.

- Result: Describe the outcome or result of your actions. Be specific about what you achieved, and if possible, use numbers or data to support your claims. Explain what you learned from the experience, and how it helped you to develop your skills and knowledge.

By using the STAR method, you can organize your thoughts, provide clear and specific examples, and demonstrate how your past experiences align with the position and company. It's a great way to showcase your skills, experience, and achievements in a clear and structured way during an interview.

Example: "Tell me about a time when you had to handle a difficult situation or conflict at work."

Situation: I was working on a large project at my previous company, and one of the key members of the team had a very different working style and communication approach than the rest of the team. This caused a lot of tension and conflict within the team, and it was affecting the progress of the project.

Task: My task was to find a way to resolve the conflict and ensure that the project was completed on time and within budget.

Action: I took the following actions to resolve the situation:

- First, I scheduled a team meeting to discuss the issue and gather everyone's perspectives on the conflict.

- I then took the time to understand the root cause of the conflict, which was mainly due to differences in communication styles and expectations.

- I then worked with the team member who was causing the conflict to come up with a plan to align our communication and working styles.

- I also set up regular check-ins and progress updates to keep everyone on the same page, and to ensure that any issues were addressed in a timely manner.

Result: As a result of my actions, the conflict was resolved, and the team was able to work together more effectively. The project was completed on time and within budget and received positive feedback from our stakeholders. Additionally, I was able to develop my conflict resolution and communication skills, and I was able to apply this knowledge to other situations in my future professional experiences.

3b. Show how your past experiences align with the position and company's goals and objectives.

Let's say you are applying for a position as an IT Executive at a company that specializes in providing healthcare solutions.

You might say something like: "In my previous role as an IT Executive at XYZ Healthcare, I was responsible for leading the digital transformation strategy for the organization. This included implementing a new EHR system, upgrading the infrastructure, and rolling out new mobile and web applications for patients and providers. I successfully led the implementation of these new technologies which resulted in a 30% increase in patient satisfaction and a 40% increase in operational efficiency. Furthermore, I also developed a cybersecurity strategy that reduced the company's risk of data breaches by 50%. These successes align directly with the goals and objectives of this position, which include implementing new technologies to improve patient satisfaction and operational efficiency, as well as ensuring the security of patient data."

You are showing the interviewer that your past experiences align with the position and company's goals and objectives by providing specific examples of how you have successfully led digital transformation initiatives and improved patient satisfaction and operational efficiency in the past. Additionally, you've also highlighted how you've reduced the risk of data breaches, which is important for a healthcare organization. This demonstrates that you have the relevant skills and experience to be successful in the role as an IT Executive.

3c. Emphasize your ability to think strategically and make decisions that align with the company's vision.

Let's say you are applying for a position as an IT Executive at a company that specializes in providing financial services.

You might say something like: "In my previous role as an IT Executive at XYZ Financial, I was responsible for leading the technology strategy for the organization. I recognized that our current technology infrastructure was not aligned with our company's vision to be a leader in digital banking services. I developed a strategic plan that involved upgrading our technology infrastructure, implementing new digital banking services, and rolling out a mobile banking app. I also made the decision to invest in artificial intelligence and machine learning technologies to improve risk management and enhance the customer experience. These decisions not only align with the company's vision of being a leader in digital banking services but also resulted in a 20% increase in customer satisfaction and a 15% increase in revenue from digital banking services."

You are showing the interviewer that you have the ability to think strategically and make decisions that align with the company's vision by providing specific examples of how you have successfully led technology initiatives that aligned with the company's vision in the past. This demonstrates that you have the relevant skills and experience to be successful in the role as an IT Executive.

3d. Highlight your leadership and team management skills, including how you have effectively led and motivated teams in the past.

Let's say you are applying for a position as an IT Executive at a company that specializes in providing e-commerce services.

You might say something like: "In my previous role as an IT Executive at XYZ e-commerce, I was responsible for leading a team of developers, designers, and QA engineers to deliver a new e-commerce platform. I effectively led the team by setting clear goals and expectations, regularly providing feedback, and coaching team members to achieve their full potential. I also implemented agile methodologies to increase collaboration and communication within the team. This resulted in a 25% increase in productivity and a 30% decrease in project completion time. Additionally, I also implemented a career development program that helped to retain top talent and reduce turnover by 50%. These successes are a testament to my ability to lead and manage teams effectively, while also ensuring they are motivated and productive."

You are showing the interviewer that you have the ability to lead and manage teams effectively by providing specific examples of how you have led a team to achieve specific goals, increase productivity and reduce turnover in the past. This demonstrates that you have the relevant skills and experience to be successful in the role as an IT Executive.

3e. Provide specific examples of how you have handled challenges and conflicts and explain the strategies you used to resolve them.

Let's say you are applying for a position as an IT Executive at a company that specializes in providing logistics services.

You might say something like: "In my previous role as an IT Executive at XYZ logistics, I was responsible for implementing a new warehouse management system. During the implementation process, I faced a significant challenge when the system's vendor failed to deliver on their promises and the project was running behind schedule and over budget.

To handle this challenge, I first identified the root cause of the problem, which was a lack of communication and cooperation from the vendor. I then developed a plan to address the issue, which included:

- Setting clear expectations and milestones with the vendor and establishing regular communication channels.

- Providing additional resources and support to the vendor to ensure that they were able to meet the project's requirements.

- Implementing a change management plan to mitigate the impact of the delay on internal stakeholders and customers.

As a result of these actions, the project was successfully completed on time and within budget and received positive feedback from internal stakeholders and customers. This experience taught me the importance of clear communication and cooperation, and how to effectively manage vendor relationships in order to achieve project success."

You are showing the interviewer that you have the ability to handle challenges and conflicts by providing specific examples of how you have handled such situations in the past and explaining the strategies you used to resolve them effectively. This demonstrates that you have the relevant skills and experience to be successful in the role as an IT Executive.

3f. Demonstrate your ability to communicate and collaborate with both technical and non-technical stakeholders.

Let's say you are applying for a position as an IT Executive at a company that specializes in providing retail services.

You might say something like: "In my previous role as an IT Executive at XYZ Retail, I was responsible for leading the implementation of a new point-of-sale system across all of the company's stores. This required me to communicate and collaborate with both technical and non-technical stakeholders, including store managers, IT staff, and vendors.

To effectively communicate and collaborate with all stakeholders, I implemented the following strategies:

- Developed clear and concise project plans and timelines to ensure everyone was aware of their roles and responsibilities.

- Set up regular meetings with store managers and IT staff to gather feedback and address any issues or concerns.

- Utilized non-technical language when communicating with non-technical stakeholders to ensure that they understood the project goals and progress.

- Provided training to store managers and IT staff to ensure they were comfortable and proficient with the new system.

As a result of these efforts, the project was completed on time, and all stakeholders were satisfied with the outcome. The new point-of-sale system led to a 15% increase in sales and a 10% decrease in errors. This experience taught me the importance of effective communication and collaboration in order to achieve success in a project that involves multiple stakeholders with different levels of technical expertise."

Here is a shorter example: I communicate technical concepts to non-technical stakeholders by using plain language and providing examples and analogies that they can understand. I also make sure to provide visual aids, such as diagrams and flowcharts, to help explain complex concepts. Additionally, I make sure to ask clarifying questions and confirm that the stakeholders understand the information before moving forward.

With both examples you are showing the interviewer that you have the ability to communicate and collaborate with both technical and non-technical stakeholders by providing specific examples of how you have done so in the past and the strategies you used to achieve successful outcomes. This demonstrates that you have the relevant skills and experience to be successful in the role as an IT Executive.

3g. Show your ability to stay current with industry trends and technologies and how you have implemented them in your past roles.

Let's say you are applying for a position as an IT Executive at a company that specializes in providing education services.

You might say something like: "In my previous role as an IT Executive at XYZ Education, I was responsible for leading the technology strategy for the organization. I made it a priority to stay current with industry trends and technologies in order to provide the best possible solutions to our students and faculty. One example of this is the implementation of a Learning Management System (LMS) that utilizes Artificial Intelligence (AI) and Machine Learning (ML) technologies to personalize the learning experience for students.

To implement this new technology, I took the following steps:

- Researched and evaluated different LMS options that utilize AI and ML technologies.

- Collaborated with faculty and students to gather requirements and feedback on the LMS.

- Led a team of developers to customize and implement the LMS to meet the specific needs of our institution.

- Provided training to faculty and staff on how to effectively use the new system.

- Continuously monitored and evaluated the system's performance and made necessary adjustments to improve the overall experience.

As a result of this implementation, we saw a 10% increase in student engagement and satisfaction, and a 15% increase in retention rates.

By staying current with industry trends and technologies, I was able to provide the best possible solutions for our students and faculty, and this experience has taught me the importance of staying current and continuously evaluating new technologies in order to provide the best solutions for the organization.

3h. Be prepared to discuss your plans for driving digital transformation and innovation within the organization.

Let's say you are applying for a position as an Executive at a company that specializes in providing transportation services.

You might say something like: "As an executive, I understand the importance of digital transformation and innovation in order to stay competitive in today's market. Based on my research and understanding of the industry, my plans for driving digital transformation and innovation within the organization include:

- Implementing a data-driven approach to decision-making by investing in data management and analytics technologies.

- Utilizing Internet of Things (IoT) technologies to optimize fleet management and improve operational efficiency.

- Developing mobile and web applications to enhance the customer experience and increase customer loyalty.

- Investing in blockchain technology to improve security and transparency in logistics and supply chain management.

- Developing a robust cybersecurity strategy to protect the company's data and assets.

These plans align with industry trends and will give the organization a competitive edge. Additionally, I am prepared to lead and drive these initiatives by working closely with internal stakeholders and external partners to ensure their success.

3i. Highlight your ability to take calculated risks and think outside the box to drive business growth and improve efficiency.

Let's say you are applying for a position as an IT Executive at a company that specializes in providing e-commerce services.

You might say something like: "In my previous role as an IT Executive at XYZ e-commerce, I was tasked with driving business growth and improving efficiency. I recognized that our current technology infrastructure was not scalable and would limit our growth potential. I took a calculated risk and proposed a new cloud-based infrastructure that would provide greater scalability and cost savings.

To make this happen, I implemented the following strategies:

- Researched and evaluated different cloud infrastructure options.

- Collaborated with the business team to understand the current and future needs of the organization.

- Developed a detailed migration plan with minimal disruption to the business operations.

- Worked closely with the development team to ensure a seamless transition to the new infrastructure.

- Continuously monitored and evaluated the performance of the new infrastructure and made necessary adjustments to improve efficiency.

As a result of this initiative, we were able to increase our online sales by 30% and reduce our IT operating costs by 20%.

This experience taught me the importance of taking calculated risks and thinking outside the box to drive business growth and improve efficiency. I am comfortable with evaluating different options and proposing new technologies that align with the company's goals and objectives.

3j. Be honest, transparent, and be willing to admit when you don't know the answer but be ready to explain how you would go about finding the answer.

Let's say you are in an interview for an IT Executive position and the interviewer asks you a question about a specific technology that you are not familiar with.

You might say something like: "I am not familiar with that specific technology, but I am always willing to learn and expand my knowledge. I would approach finding the answer in the following way:

- First, I would conduct research to understand the basics of the technology and its potential use cases.

- I would then seek out experts in the field and ask for their input and advice.

- I would also look for any relevant case studies or success stories to gain a better understanding of how the technology has been implemented in the past.

- Once I have a solid understanding of the technology and its potential benefits, I would present my findings to the relevant stakeholders and make a recommendation on how it could be implemented in our organization.

I believe that being honest and transparent about my knowledge and willingness to seek out answers is important in any executive role. I am always willing to admit when I don't know something, but I am also committed to finding the answer and making informed decisions. In this specific case, I would make sure to stay updated on the technology and its developments, and continuously evaluate its potential benefits and implementation in our organization. Additionally, I would also make sure to communicate my progress and findings to the relevant stakeholders and involve them in the decision-making process."

By being honest, transparent and willing to admit when you don't know the answer and have a clear plan of action to find the answer, it demonstrates your ability to be resourceful and proactive in finding solutions, it also shows your humility and willingness to learn. This is an important skill for an IT executive, as the technology landscape is constantly evolving and it's important to be able to adapt and stay current with the latest trends and technologies.

Ch. 4 IT Executive Specific Interview Questions and Example Answers

4a. Can you tell us about your experience leading and managing technology projects?

Provide specific examples of projects you have led, the technologies and methodologies used, and the outcomes achieved. Emphasize your ability to manage timelines, resources, and stakeholders.

Example answer:

I have over 10 years of experience leading and managing technology projects in various industries. One of my most notable projects was leading the implementation of a new CRM system for a retail company. I managed a team of developers and worked closely with key stakeholders to understand their needs and develop a solution that met their requirements. The project was completed on time and within budget and resulted in a 20% increase in sales for the company.

4b. How do you stay up to date with the latest technologies and trends in the industry?

Mention your professional development activities, such as attending conferences, taking online courses, or staying active in professional organizations. Explain how you use this knowledge to stay current and identify opportunities for your organization.

Example answer: I stay up to date with the latest technologies and trends by attending industry conferences, taking online courses, and following technology publications and blogs. I also participate in professional organizations, such as the Association for Computing Machinery, which keeps me informed about new developments in the field.

4c. Can you tell us about a particularly challenging problem you had to solve and how you approached it?

Provide a specific example of a difficult problem you faced and how you approached it, highlighting your problem-solving and analytical skills. Be sure to mention the outcome and the results achieved.

Example answer: One of the most challenging problems I had to solve was during a project where the team was struggling to meet deadlines. I identified that the issue was poor communication and lack of clear project management. To address this, I implemented daily stand-up meetings, and established a clear project management process that included detailed timelines and regular progress reports. This helped the team to stay on track and we were able to deliver the project on time.

4d. Can you walk us through your leadership style and how you motivate your team?

Describe your leadership style, focusing on how you empower and motivate your team to achieve results. Provide specific examples of how you have led and motivated a team in the past.

Example answer: My leadership style is a combination of mentoring and empowering my team members. I believe in giving my team members the autonomy to make decisions while also providing guidance and support when needed. I also make sure to recognize and reward good work and provide regular feedback to help team members improve and grow.

4e. How do you prioritize and manage competing demands on your time and resources?

Describe your approach to prioritizing and managing competing demands, using specific examples from your experience. Emphasize your ability to make sound decisions in a fast-paced and dynamic environment.

Example answer: I prioritize and manage competing demands by setting clear goals and objectives for each project, and regularly reviewing progress. I also use tools such as Gantt charts and project management software to help me stay organized and on top of deadlines.

4f. Can you give an example of a successful project you led and what you believe contributed to its success?

Provide a specific example of a successful project you led and explain what you believe contributed to its success, highlighting your leadership and management skills.

Example answer: One of the most successful projects I led was the implementation of a new ERP system for a manufacturing company. The project was a success because of my ability to effectively communicate with all stakeholders, including the C-suite, the IT department, and end-users. I also made sure that the project team was well-equipped and well-trained, which contributed to the smooth implementation of the system. I also established a clear project management process that ensured all tasks were completed on time and within budget. Additionally, by involving all stakeholders in the decision-making process, I was able to ensure buy-in from everyone and mitigate any resistance to the change.

4g. How do you ensure that your team is meeting its objectives and delivering results?

Describe your approach to setting and monitoring objectives, providing specific examples of how you have ensured that your team is meeting its objectives and delivering results in the past.

Example answer: I ensure that my team is meeting its objectives by setting clear goals and objectives, and regularly monitoring progress. I provide regular feedback and coaching to team members and recognize and reward good performance. I also ensure that team members have the necessary training and resources to perform their roles effectively. I also regularly review processes and procedures to identify areas for improvement and implement changes as needed.

4h. How do you communicate technical concepts to non-technical stakeholders?

Provide an example of a time when you had to explain a technical concept to a non-technical person. Explain how you approached the task and what methods you used to make the information understandable and actionable.

Example answer: I communicate technical concepts to non-technical stakeholders by using plain language and providing examples and analogies that they can understand. I also make sure to provide visual aids, such as diagrams and flowcharts, to help explain complex concepts. Additionally, I make sure to ask clarifying questions and confirm that the stakeholders understand the information before moving forward.

4i. Can you provide an example of a situation where you had to make a difficult decision and how you approached it?

Provide an example of a difficult decision you had to make and explain how you approached it. Highlight your ability to weigh risks and benefits and make sound decisions under pressure.

Example answer: One situation where I had to make a difficult decision was when a key team member was underperforming. After evaluating the situation, I decided that the best course of action was to provide additional training and coaching to the team member to help improve their performance. However, if there was no improvement, I would have to let them go. I approached the situation by first gathering all the facts and considering all possible options before making a decision.

4j. How do you plan and implement changes in an organization's technology strategy?

Describe your approach to developing and implementing changes in an organization's technology strategy. Provide specific examples of how you have done this in the past, highlighting your ability to think strategically and lead organizational change.

Example answer: I plan and implement changes in an organization's technology strategy by first conducting a thorough analysis of the current technology landscape and identifying areas for improvement. I then involve key stakeholders in the decision-making process and develop a plan that aligns with the overall business strategy. I also make sure to communicate the plan clearly to all stakeholders and involve them in the implementation process to ensure buy-in and minimize resistance to change.

4k. Can you tell us about a time when you had to manage a crisis or unexpected event in a project?

Provide an example of a crisis or unexpected event you had to manage and explain how you approached it, highlighting your ability to think quickly and manage pressure. Be sure to mention the outcome and the results achieved.

Example answer: One time when I had to manage a crisis was when a server went down during a critical project. I quickly assessed the situation and identified the root cause of the problem. I then established a plan of action and communicated it to the team and worked with the IT department to get the server back online as quickly as possible. I also kept all stakeholders informed of the situation and the steps being taken to resolve it. Through effective communication and quick decision making, we were able to minimize the impact of the crisis and get the project back on track.

4l. How do you ensure the security and integrity of an organization's data and systems?

Describe your approach to data and system security, including specific steps you take to protect sensitive information and comply with regulations and standards.

Example answer: I manage and mitigate security risks in technology projects by conducting regular security assessments and implementing security controls such as firewalls, intrusion detection systems, and encryption. I also make sure that all team members are trained on security best practices and that there is a clear process in place for reporting and responding to security incidents.

4j. How do you manage and evaluate vendor relationships and partnerships?

Describe your approach to managing vendor relationships and partnerships.

Example answer: I foster a culture of innovation and creativity within my team by encouraging open communication and collaboration, and providing opportunities for team members to share ideas and give feedback. I also make sure to recognize and reward good ideas and provide resources for team members to explore and develop new technologies and ideas.

4k. Can you discuss a project where you had to navigate and overcome political or organizational obstacles?

Provide an example of a project where you had to navigate and overcome political or organizational obstacles. Explain how you approached the situation and what methods you used to build support and overcome resistance.

Example answer: One project where I had to navigate political obstacles was when I was leading the implementation of a new system for a government agency. The project was met with resistance from certain departments who felt that the new system would disrupt their processes. To overcome this, I made sure to involve all stakeholders in the decision-making process and address their concerns. I also established a clear communication plan to keep everyone informed of the project progress and benefits. Through effective stakeholder management, I was able to build support and successfully implement the new system.

4l. How do you stay current with industry regulations and standards?

Mention your professional development activities, such as attending seminars, training, or staying active in professional organizations. Explain how you use this knowledge to stay current and identify opportunities for your organization.

Example answer: I stay current with industry regulations and standards by regularly attending seminars and training, and staying active in professional organizations such as ISO and NIST. I also make sure to read industry publications and stay informed about new developments in the field.

4m. How do you approach budgeting and financial management for technology projects?

Describe your approach to budgeting and financial management for technology projects, including specific steps you take to ensure that projects are completed on time and within budget. Provide examples of your budget management experience.

Example answer: I approach budgeting and financial management for technology projects by first developing a clear project plan that includes timelines, milestones, and budgets. I also regularly review project progress and adjust the budget as needed to ensure that the project stays within budget. I also make sure to have a clear process in place for tracking and reporting expenses.

4n. Can you discuss a time when you had to make a difficult personnel decision?

Provide an example of a difficult personnel decision you had to make and explain how you approached it. Highlight your ability to make sound decisions while balancing the needs of the organization and the individual employee.

Example answer: I once had to make a difficult personnel decision when a team member was not meeting performance expectations. After evaluating the situation and providing coaching and training, it became clear that the individual was not a good fit for the team. I approached the situation by having a direct and honest conversation with the team member, and ultimately had to let them go. It was a difficult decision, but it was necessary to ensure the success of the project.

4o. How do you handle conflicts or disagreements within a team?

Describe your approach to handling conflicts or disagreements within a team, including specific steps you take to resolve conflicts in a fair and effective manner.

Example answer: I handle conflicts or disagreements within a team by first identifying the root cause of the conflict and then facilitating open and honest communication among all parties involved. I make sure that everyone has an opportunity to express their perspective and concerns. I also make sure to remain neutral and find a solution that is fair and beneficial for all parties involved.

4p. How do you measure and communicate the ROI of technology projects?

Describe your approach to measuring and communicating the ROI of technology projects, including specific metrics you use and methods you use to communicate results to stakeholders.

Example answer: I measure and communicate the ROI of technology projects by first identifying and agreeing on key metrics with stakeholders. These metrics may include productivity improvements, cost savings, and increased revenue. I then track these metrics throughout the project and provide regular reports to stakeholders on the project's progress and ROI and the ROI achieved. I also make sure to communicate the ROI in a clear and understandable way, using both quantitative data and qualitative examples. I also make sure to communicate the ROI not just in financial terms but also in terms of other benefits such as improved customer satisfaction or increased efficiency.

4q. Can you discuss a time when you had to implement a new technology or system within an organization?

Provide an example of a time when you had to implement a new technology or system within an organization. Explain how you approached the task, the challenges you faced, and how you overcame them.

Example answer: I once had to work with a vendor who was not meeting their commitments and was causing delays in the project. I approached the situation by first having a direct and honest conversation with the vendor to understand the root cause of the problem. I then worked with them to establish clear communication and expectations, and set up regular progress check-ins. I also made sure to document any issues and work with them to find solutions. Through effective communication and problem-solving, we were able to get the vendor back on track and deliver the project successfully.

4r. How do you approach risk management for technology projects?

To answer this question, provide an example of a project where you have successfully aligned technology with the business strategy. Explain the steps you took to involve key stakeholders, align project objectives with business goals, and how you regularly reviewed progress to ensure alignment.

Example answer: I approach risk management by identifying potential risks early on in the project and developing a plan to mitigate or manage them. I regularly review the project progress and update the risk management plan as needed. I also ensure that there is a clear process in place for identifying and reporting new risks as they arise.

4s. How do you handle resistance to change within an organization?

To answer this question, provide an example of a project where you have effectively built and maintained relationships with key stakeholders. Explain the steps you took to communicate and involve stakeholders, keep them informed, and take their feedback into account.

Example answer: I understand that change can be difficult for some people, so I take a collaborative approach to managing resistance. I involve key stakeholders in the change process and involve them in the decision-making process. I also ensure that clear communication channels are in place to address any concerns or issues that arise. I also make sure that the benefits of the change are clearly communicated to all stakeholders.

4t. Can you discuss a time when you had to balance conflicting priorities?

To answer this question, provide an example of a situation where you have successfully evaluated and improved the performance of your team. Explain the steps you took to set clear goals, provide feedback and coaching, and review processes and procedures for improvement.

Example answer: I once had to manage a project that required me to balance the needs of different stakeholders with competing priorities. I found a way to establish clear communication channels with all stakeholders and set realistic expectations. I also made sure that the project team was aware of the various priorities and how they fit into the overall project plan. By involving all stakeholders in the process, I was able to balance their needs and deliver a successful project.

4u. How do you ensure that technology projects align with the overall business strategy?

The interviewer is looking for an answer that demonstrates your ability to align technology projects with the overall business strategy. They want to see that you understand the importance of involving key stakeholders in the decision-making process, that you have a clear understanding of the business objectives, and that you have the skills and experience to develop a project plan that aligns with those objectives.

They also want to see that you have a systematic approach to ensure alignment throughout the project. This includes regular reviews of project progress, making adjustments as needed, and keeping stakeholders informed of progress and alignment to the business objectives.

They also want to see that you have experience in aligning a technology project with the business strategy, and that you understand the importance of involving all stakeholders in the decision-making process. They also want to see that you have the ability to think strategically and that you can develop a plan that aligns with the overall business strategy.

Example answer: To ensure that technology projects align with the overall business strategy, I make sure to involve key stakeholders, such as the C-suite and business leaders, in the decision-making process from the outset. I also make sure to understand the overall business objectives and goals and align the project objectives with those goals. I also establish a clear project plan that includes timelines, milestones, and budgets. Additionally, I make sure to regularly review project progress and adjust the plan as needed to ensure alignment with the overall business strategy. This includes conducting regular progress review meeting with the stakeholders and updating them on the progress of the project and how it aligns with the business objectives.

4v. How do you build and maintain relationships with key stakeholders?

To answer this question, provide an example of a time when you have successfully handled a crisis or incident. Explain the steps you took to have a clear plan in place, identify key stakeholders, and communicate and escalate the incident effectively.

Example answer: I build and maintain relationships with key stakeholders by regularly communicating with them and involving them in the project planning and decision-making process. I also make sure to keep them informed of project progress and any issues that arise. I also make sure that I am responsive to their needs and concerns, and that their feedback is taken into account.

4w. How do you evaluate and improve the performance of your team?

To answer this question, provide an example of a situation where you have successfully managed and mitigated vendor and third-party risks. Explain the steps you took to perform due diligence, establish clear contracts and agreements, and keep open lines of communication.

Example answer: I evaluate and improve the performance of my team by setting clear goals and objectives, and regularly monitoring progress. I provide regular feedback and coaching to team members and recognize and reward good performance. I also ensure that team members have the necessary training and resources to perform their roles effectively. I also regularly review processes and procedures to identify areas for improvement and implement changes as needed.

4x. Can you discuss a time when you had to work with a difficult team member?

To answer this question, provide an example of a project where you had to comply with multiple regulations and standards. Explain the steps you took to understand and apply the regulations, and how you ensured compliance throughout the project.

Example answer: I once had to work with a team member who had a different communication style and approach to work than the rest of the team. I addressed the issue by having open and honest conversations with the team member to understand their perspective and concerns. I also set clear expectations for communication and collaboration within the team. I also provided regular feedback and coaching to help the team member improve their performance and work effectively with the rest of the team.

4y. How do you approach crisis communication and incident management?

To answer this question, provide an example of a time when you have successfully planned and implemented changes in an organization's technology strategy. Explain the steps you took to conduct a thorough analysis of the current technology landscape, involve key stakeholders in the decision-making process, develop a plan that aligns with the overall business strategy, and communicate the plan clearly to all stakeholders.

Example answer: I approach crisis communication and incident management by having a clear plan in place for dealing with unexpected events or crises. This includes identifying key stakeholders and developing a communication plan for keeping them informed. I also make sure that there is a clear process for reporting and escalating incidents, and that the necessary resources are in place to respond quickly and effectively.

4z. How do you manage and mitigate vendor and third-party risks?

To answer this question, provide an example of a time when you have successfully handled resistance to change within an organization. Explain the steps you took to understand and address concerns, involve stakeholders in the decision-making process, and communicate the benefits and value of the change.

Example answer: I manage and mitigate vendor and third-party risks by performing thorough due diligence on potential vendors and regularly reviewing their performance. I also make sure that clear contracts and agreements are in place to define expectations and responsibilities. I also keep open lines of communication with vendors to address any issues that arise and to ensure they are aligned with the overall goals and objectives of the organization.

4zz. Can you discuss a time when you had to navigate a complex regulatory environment?

To answer this question, provide an example of a time when you have successfully balanced conflicting priorities and managed competing demands. Explain the steps you took to set clear goals and objectives, prioritize tasks, and use tools and techniques such as Gantt charts and project management software to stay organized and on top of deadlines.

Example answer: I once had to lead a project that required compliance with multiple regulations and standards. I made sure that I had a clear understanding of the regulations and standards and how they applied to the project. I also made sure that the project team was aware of the regulations and how to comply with them.

Ch. 5 Non-Specific Interview Questions and Example Answers

5a. Tell us about yourself.

A lot of jobs require someone who can think on their feet or present ideas with crispness and clarity. This question provides employers with an early preview of your core skills, your personality, and your ability to respond to an unstructured question.

This is something you'll be asked a lot at the beginning of an interview. Here are three tips that'll help you nail the opener.

Be succinct, honest, and engaging. Resist the urge to give a detailed account of the last two decades of your career. The interviewer is looking for an answer that shows them you're qualified and can respond to an unstructured question.

Use the job description to prepare. Reread what they want and highlight the most required skills that you have. Are they looking for someone who can solve problems or deal with tough customers? Pick a few and brainstorm how you can describe yourself while showcasing your strengths for what they're seeking.

Tie your story to their needs. People love a good tale, so weave in some personality. For example, maybe you fell in love with the hospitality industry because your grandparents ran a bed and breakfast. Connect your story back to the job, keep it short, and be truthful.

Tips

- Prepare for this question in advance and have a compelling story about your past experiences.
- Pull prominent skills from the job description.
- Be (succinct, honest, and engaging).

Example answer: From a very early age I've been a problem solver. I was that kid who would take apart anything so I could see how it worked—and then try to put it back together.

As you can imagine, it drove my parents nuts. But even though I tortured my family at times, the tinkering trait has served me well in my career.

After graduating from Purdue, I was recruited into a field technician job and got paid to take apart broken packaging equipment. It was like living the dream.

That job also made me realize I'm really good with difficult customers, and that's what helped me land my current account manager role.

While I love my job and have been successful in it, it has moved me away from the manufacturing floor. Now, the reason I'm so interested in this position is that it seems to provide a really great blend of one-on-one work with clients and hands-on problem solving.

Why this answer worked well:

- He gave a vivid image of his childhood home and told a memorable story about it.
- He picked two prominent required skills from the job description, problem solving and customer service, and built this interesting narrative around it.
- He showed how his career successfully evolved before he was even asked about that.
-

5b. What is your greatest strength?

Employers want to see if you can strike the right balance between confidence and humility. Hiring managers also want to get a sense for how self-aware and honest you are and align your strengths to the role at hand.

When responding to this question, you want to sound humble and not like you're arrogant or bragging. Here are some tips to help you give them a great answer.

Describe a relevant experience. If you're applying for a sales job, tell a story about a time where you helped a customer solve a problem with your solution.

Give specific details. Tell them about a time you closed a deal that helped you hit a percentage of your annual number. When you share those facts with them, it helps them visualize how effective you have been.

Show them you're a well-rounded person. For example, share a story of when you used a "soft" skill, like effective communication with a coworker, and then one about you using a technical skill, which could be anything asked for in the job description.

Tips

- Be authentic - don't make up strengths that you think the employer wants to hear.
- Tell a story about a work experience.
- Be sure the strengths you share are aligned to the role you want.

Example answer: My greatest strength is strategic thinking. I am often able to quickly spot patterns and issues and create alternatives before my teammates even realize there is an issue.

The way this shows up in my work experience is through risk mitigation. As an example, I was starting a new project with a new team in an industry I had never worked in before. The team seemed to think that the project was very straight-forward and that they didn't even really need a project manager to help them.

We kicked off the project by creating a charter, social contract, and reviewing the risks. We got halfway through the project and realized the requirements were ambiguous and we weren't delivering what the client really wanted. I had picked up on some subtle cues that this was the case and had already taken the initiative to meet with the client to clarify the requirements.

I presented my findings to the team and showed three alternatives to our existing plan to accommodate the updated requirements. From my team's point of view, I was able to bring solutions to the problem conversation and we didn't lose any time with the project timeline. It was a win win!

Why this answer worked well:

- The candidate demonstrated the ability to detect issues and opportunities early.
- The example showed a willingness to take initiative to improve clarity and process.

Quick example answer: Communication. I always try to understand other people's perceptions. We all perceive situations differently. A lot of conflicts are merely caused by people's perceptions being different. Spending a little extra time to try and understand where someone is coming from can greatly reduce tensions and misunderstandings.

5c. What is your greatest weakness?

The interviewer is assessing whether your weaknesses will get in the way of doing the job. Employers are looking for humility and whether you're committed to learning and growing. This is a place you can showcase what you're doing to improve.

This can feel like a tricky question, but it's a good opportunity to shine. Here are some tips on how to answer:

Be humble. You want to communicate an authentic story that shows you're self-aware. It's okay that you don't come off as perfect, that's authentic, which is important for someone who will have to trust you in the role that they're hiring for.

Choose a trait that is not too relevant to the job. For example, if you're applying for a project manager role, choose a weakness that is more related to creativity, which is something that doesn't disqualify you from the description of the things that would make someone successful in that role.

Show how you manage it. Have a fix-it strategy. For example, if you struggle with remembering product details so you track them in their phone or side notebook, that's okay, share that with them. That shows that you've got commitment to solving that problem and addressing it.

Tips

- Employers are looking for self-awareness and personal accountability.

- It's good to be honest about what you're not great at.

- Share what you are doing to actively improve on this weakness.

Example answer: I have a strong desire to succeed, which generally serves me well. But I've realized that it can also be a blind spot if I'm not being honest with myself about what's possible.

A few years ago, I was working on a remote control, and the schedule was very tight. We were trying to go from concept to mass production in six months, and there was a high amount of pressure.

I made the decision to continue with the factory build, even though my team was concerned that one of the parts we were using would fail. Because we had already spent $200,000 on the factory process, I pushed ahead. I was afraid to tell the program managers that we wouldn't be able to hit our targets. Eventually, I was forced to — but I had already lost the company money.

What I learned from this is the importance of being honest right up front and being realistic, even if it's not the outcome I want. I've learned that failures can be turned around more easily when addressed quickly.

Now I communicate status with program managers on a weekly basis. I always make them aware of the risks and what the impact might be. In the past four years, we haven't missed a single delivery.

Why this answer worked well:

- The answer provided an honest self-review with a clear example that took the interviewer through the decision-making process.

- The candidate took accountability and specific steps to prevent another issue.

Quick example answer: Impatience is my greatest weakness. It's cause me some problems. But impatience is also something that's driven me to succeed faster than other people.

5d. Why should we hire you?

This question tests how persuasive you are. Interviewers want to see if you can make a calm, confident case for yourself, even if they're acting skeptical. They're looking for factual and compelling answers.

This is a nerve-racking question, so make sure you're set up for success. Here are some tips that can help you do well in answering it.

Ask yourself why you think you're qualified. Prepare for the interview by picking three or four qualifications and experiences that help them understand why you're a fit for this job.

Tell them how you'd fit in. Paint a picture of what you'd accomplish that gives you a leg up on the competition. Also, show them why you are a great match for this company by letting them see that you know about their mission, their vision, how they operate—and how you would fit into that really well.

Speak authentically. How you say something is as important as what you say. So, when you're sharing your successes and you're answering these questions, speak like the best version of yourself and make sure that you're doing it in a way that allows the interviewers to connect to you.

Tips

- Start with the three or four best reasons you've got.

- Cite results, credentials, and other people's praise so you don't seem self-absorbed.

- Be concise and invite follow-up questions at the end.

Example answer: My resume demonstrates that I've been successful with the key responsibilities of this role: managing teams, developing strategic sales plans, and delivering quarterly targets.

I've been managing teams for the last 10 years and to this day, many of my former direct reports still call and ask for career or personal advice.

I've also led the development of strategic plans with the customer for years. I first listen and understand their priorities and objectives, then develop a win-win solution for both parties.

Last year my team received 2 awards. The first was from our

internal organization for collaboration and partnership in developing our 3-year plans. The second was the Vendor of The Year Award from the customer for putting together plans that exceeded their growth targets.

I've been in sales for the last 15 years and I know how important it is to hit targets — it's the lifeblood of what we do. That's why I work hard to support and guide my team, as well as work with internal partners to anticipate and remove roadblocks.

I believe I would be a great fit for this role as I already have relevant experience and been successful in my previous roles.

Why this answer worked well:

- The answer detailed deep industry knowledge and a record of success across several themes.

- The focus on teams painted a picture of an invested leader who sees success as collective.

5e. Why do you want to work here?

Interviewers want to understand what prompted you to apply for this job. They don't want candidates who are indifferent to where they work. Instead, they want someone who offers very specific reasons for why they want this job.

You would be amazed by how few people get this question right. So, you've got a big opportunity to shine.

Make it all about them. Your best answer will be about what they need. It'll show that you've done your research and have thought through what you can contribute to that team.

Show them how you can help. Weave your story into the context of what you can contribute. If you have strong accounting skills and are interviewing for a finance role at a humane society, you could suggest that this job would allow you to blend your professional skills with your passion for animals.

Speak from the heart. Telling a genuine story can make a big difference. For example, I once worked with a client who was applying for a zoo event manager job, and she had grown up next door to that zoo and had great memories of the peacocks flying over the fence and sitting on her dad's car. So, her answer was that she wanted people to have fun memories of that zoo just like she did. Try to top that.

Tips

- Make it about them first.

- Show you've done your research.

- Use this as a key opportunity to outshine the competition.

- Speak from the heart.

5f. Why do you want to leave your current role?

Hiring managers will often ask this question, and it's a test. Are you running away from something, or are you running towards something? The advice when you get this question is simple:

Stay positive. Employers want to see that you have a good attitude in general. Resist the temptation to say bad things about your current job, employer, or boss.

Focus on where you'd like to go. You should come off as

someone who is looking forward, not backward. Portray your interests more in the light of what you want to get out of your next role.

Bring it back to them. Show them that you've done your homework about their company and relate what you tell them back to the specific job you're interviewing for.

Tips

- Don't talk negatively about past roles or former bosses - employers don't want to work with people who complain.

- Be gracious when things haven't worked out in the past.

- Share some of the ways you're working on improving.

5g. Tell me about something you've accomplished that you are proud of.

Respond to this kind of question with a compelling story that uses the "SAR" framework: situation, action, and results.

Describe the situation. Talk about the initial events that occurred. What were the problems that you were experiencing? What needed to be solved and what resources did you have--or not have? This is a key part of the story, so it should be about three to four sentences long.

Get into the action. Speak about the key milestones that you went through. Tell them what you did to turn the situation around. Don't go into too much detail though. It should only be about two to three sentences, and try to use active verbs, things like "I implemented" or "I persuaded".

Show the results. Let them know how well things turned out, how the problems were solved and what you may have learned along the way. Try to include a clincher at the end, like dollars saved or improved profitability. It drives home that you did a great thing.

Tips

- Describe the problem that existed before you took action.

- Talk about how you took initiative to solve the problem.

- Explain why you are proud of the outcome and what would have happened if you hadn't stepped in.

5h. What are your salary expectations?

This is a question you'll get all too often, so here are a few tips to help you master the answer:

Give them a salary range. Let them know there's room to negotiate (instead of starting with a specific number). Avoid going too low though because that's going to work against your interests. And don't go too high either, or you may freeze yourself out of the opportunity.

Do some neutral research. Give them a reasonable place to start from. You can use a resource like the LinkedIn Salary Tool to find out what other companies are paying people in this role and share with them what you learned about this salary range. Then they'll have to base their compensation at least on those numbers because you've let them know what other similar organizations are giving to employees who do that job.

Bring up signing bonuses. Doing this can create a win-win situation for both parties. At the end of a negotiation, asking for extra money up top is often a way to bridge the gap between what you want and what you're being offered.

Tips

- Know the industry norms for similar jobs.

- Talk about ranges, rather than exact numbers.

- Make the case that you offer premium value.

5i. What do you like to do outside of work?

With this question, employers are looking to get a feel for your likability and cultural fit. So, what should you say—and not say? Here are a few tips.

Pick one of your favorites. Go ahead and share something about your hobbies, volunteer work, or the places you enjoy traveling to. Maybe you're taking classes to help you accelerate your skills. In general, you just want to tell them something that's true and will paint you as an interesting, healthy, or good human being.

Keep it short. For example, if you're a bird watcher in your free time, skip the 22-minute account of every species you've ever documented. Share enthusiastically so your passion shines through, but don't ramble on endlessly. Doing so might give the people to whom you're trying to make a good impression the feeling that you're nervous or that brevity just isn't your strong suit.

Stick to appropriate topics. Avoid anything that might be pulverizing or offends somebody who's not a part of a particular group like politics or religion. Choose something uncontroversial or beneficial and take advantage of the opportunity to show them that you're the complete package.

Tips

- Share something that paints a favorable picture.

- Keep it short and sweet.

- Don't bore them with long stories.

- Steer clear of the inappropriate zone.

5j. Describe your leadership style.

This is a question you'll hear a lot and answering with authenticity is key. Here are three tips I have to help you get started:

Be clear about your leadership style. Don't be vague or ambivalent. If you're a team builder, say so. If you're tough, but fair, own it. Be very concise and clear on how you define your leadership so that they know very well what you're all about.

Give a detailed example that highlights it. Talk about a situation, a problem, or an obstacle, and then walk through what did you do and what was the result. What did it mean to your organization, company, and the customer? And be sure to include how you brought your team along, because this isn't all about you.

Show situations where you've adapted. Life's not going to be simple. People want to see how you've grown and changed given the situation. Just like you look for that in the people you're going to hire, the same thing with the hiring manager who's looking to hire you.

Tips

- Start by framing your basic style in a few words.

- Give an example of your leadership style in action.

- Show that you can adapt well to unexpected situations.

5k. Tell me how you handle conflict at work.

In life it's impossible to avoid conflict. A successful executive will have a method for handling it to minimize the conflict negatively impacting the business.

Example answer: Staying calm is always my first response. Sometimes it's necessary to remove myself from the situation temporarily to avoid its escalating, and then return to work to resolve the root cause. Communication and understanding other perspectives is always the key to resolving conflict.

5l. What is important to you in a work environment?

Another question to find out if you're a good fit for their environment.

Example answer: I like to be surrounded by colleagues

who are intelligent, and very passionate and energized about what they do. This fuels my energy levels and helps me perform at my peak.

5m. How do you get the best out of people?

Example answer: I believe in leading by example. There is not something I would ask someone to do that I would not do myself.

5n. How do you delegate responsibility?

Example answer: I consider the strengths of my staff and their current responsibilities. I speak with each staff member, or a small team, about what I think they could take on and how I can support them. Once I feel that they are comfortable with the task and understand what is required, I pass it on to the project manager and provide regular check-ins and support.

5o. Describe the relationship that should exist between a supervisor and those reporting to him/her.

Example answer: The most important thing is to establish a relationship that is based on mutual respect. The subordinate has to respect the supervisor's ability to manage, and the supervisor has to respect the employee. It should be a relationship where there is open communication between the parties. It is also important that each person knows their role and what is expected of them in order to meet objectives.

5p. Do you consider yourself a leader?

Example answer: I do consider myself a leader. I am always ready to share my expertise and provide counsel to those who are learning. When there is a new project or initiative underway, I have volunteered to take the lead and steer the project.

5q. Would you rather be liked or feared?

Example answer: I would want to be liked because I am a respected leader who leads by example. As an effective leader, my team would be fearful of not doing their best because each would know that everyone has put in a great effort, and no one wants to disappoint the team.

5r. What do you find are the most difficult decisions to make?

Example answer: The most difficult decisions are the ones that affect the lives of people. Most decisions that an executive would make have a major impact on the lives of workers. I give much weight to this fact when considering the best course of action.

5s. How would you show your team the importance of cooperation?

Example answer: I'm a data driven person and I would

create a chart that compares what we can do separately compared to what we could accomplish together to meet objectives. It is hard to think outside of ourselves, but when a person sees a visual of how he/she can work most effectively in a group, it is memorable.

5t. What qualities make you a good leader?

Example answer: I lead by example. I wouldn't ask my team to do anything that I wouldn't do. I am resourceful. I can work within a budget and time constraints to get the job done. I am also a natural teacher. I am patient and enjoy teaching people ways to work more effectively.

5u. What systems would you put in place to enable employees to give management suggestions?

Example answer: Employee feedback is essential as these are the people on the ground who can give you the best suggestions. Some employees are intimidated, or fear reprisal, no matter how much you say that you are open to feedback. It is important to have multiple ways to gain insight. I have an open-door policy where employees can speak to me at any time.

5v. Tell me about your 30,60,90 day plan if we hire you.

A 30-60-90 day plan is a roadmap for the first three months on the job, and can be a helpful way for a new hire to hit the ground running and make a positive impact quickly. When crafting a plan for an executive IT position, some key areas to consider might include:

30 Days:

- Familiarizing myself with the company's IT systems, processes, and policies

- Meeting with key stakeholders to understand their needs and priorities

- Conducting a review of the current IT infrastructure and identifying any immediate areas for improvement

60 Days:

- Developing a detailed IT strategy and roadmap for the next year, in collaboration with the leadership team and relevant departments

- Implementing any high-priority projects or initiatives identified in the review conducted in the first 30 days

- Building relationships with key vendors and partners

90 Days:

- Evaluating the success of the IT strategy and making any necessary adjustments

- Gathering feedback from team members and stakeholders on the effectiveness of the new systems and processes

- Identifying opportunities for ongoing learning and development for myself and the IT team.

Overall, the goal of this plan would be to quickly get up to speed on the current IT landscape and priorities, and to begin driving strategic initiatives that support the overall goals of the organization.

5w. Do you have any questions for me?

The way you respond to this question shows employers if you're engaged, intelligent and interested. Here are some tips on how to answer:

Show them you're paying attention. It's important to let them know you've been listening. You may want to take notes as the interview unfolds and then loop back to something you'd like to delve further into like an aspect of the job, the team, or the challenges that lie ahead.

Let them know you're excited. While being qualified for the job is essential, showing passion for their products, brand or industry takes it to the next level. So maybe you can ask a question about one of your favorite products they make or see how they're responding to an industry trend.

Get them talking about their careers. People love talking about themselves and appreciate when you notice the interesting things they're doing. For example, you can ask them how they got from Job X to Job Y, or how their work as a musician helped them in their current career. People hire people that they like and who seem genuinely interested in the role.

Tips

- Come prepared with 3-5 thoughtful questions.

- Ask questions that show you're engaged, intelligent and interested.

- Avoid no-brainer questions or ones related to salary / benefits.

Example questions to ask:

1) What do you like most about working for this organization?
2) What characteristics are most important when you consider candidates for this role?
3) What advice would you give someone coming into this role?

Final Word

It's important to note that the best answer to any interview question will depend on your own experience and qualifications. However, by providing specific examples and highlighting your qualifications, experience, and skills, you can effectively communicate your suitability for the role.

You should now be ready to ace the executive IT interview! I wish the best of luck to you and don't forget to always send a thank you email to whom you interviewed with. This should be sent within 24 hours of leaving an interview.

About the Author

Matt Olivier is an IT professional, programmer, author, and educator specializing in IT networks and cybersecurity.

He has been involved in IT since the 1990's and has been part of the rapid advancements in computer science over the last few decades.

Matt's other books available on Amazon:
1) Upgrade: Your enterprise IT
2) Cyber Security Disasters

www.ingramcontent.com/pod-product-compliance
Lightning Source LLC
LaVergne TN
LVHW051614050326
832903LV00033B/4501